MARGO

Len Jenkin

BROADWAY PLAY PUBLISHING INC
56 E 81st St., NY NY 10028-0202
212 772-8334 fax: 212 772-8358
BroadwayPlayPubl.com

MARGO VEIL
© Copyright 2008 by Len Jenkin

First printing: April 2008
I S B N: 0-88145-303-X

Book design: Marie Donovan
Word processing: Microsoft Word
Typographic controls: Ventura Publisher
Typeface: Palatino
Printed and bound in the U S A

ABOUT THE AUTHOR

Len Jenkin is a playwright, screenwriter, novelist and director. His works for the stage include DARK RIDE, MY UNCLE SAM, LIMBO TALES, LIKE I SAY, CARELESS LOVE, and THE DREAM EXPRESS. His films include *Blame it On The Night, Welcome to Oblivion*, and *American Notes*. His works have been produced throughout the United States, as well as in England, Germany, Denmark, France and Japan. His novels include *New Jerusalem, N Judah*, and *The Secret Life of Billie's Uncle Myron*.

He has been the recipient of many honors and awards, including three OBIE awards for directing and playwriting, a Guggenheim Fellowship, a nomination for an EMMY award, and four National Endowment for the Arts Fellowships. He is currently a Professor in the Dramatic Writing Department, Tisch School of the Arts, New York University.

MARGO VEIL was first produced by the Flea Theater in New York City (Carol Ostrow and Jim Simpson, Producers), opening on 20 March 2005. The company (all playing multiple roles) and creative contributors were:

Heather Christian
Michael Grenhum
Aaron Fili
Benjamin Ellis Fine
David Marcus
Lauren McCord
Julie Shavers
Lisa Sauber

Director	Len Jenkin
Set	Sue Rees
Lights	Andrew Hill
Sound	John Kilgore
Costumes	Michelle Phillips
Musical direction	Heather Christian

The play can be performed with a few as eight actors: four men and four women.

Any sound effects (trains, cars, translation machines, fog, etc) should be created live by the actors where possible.

The NARRATOR *is a role played by a number of actors. Who plays this part, and at what point in the action, should be dictated by the casting and staging of the particular production.*

The author's admiration, thanks, and apologies to all those masters of early radio. My ear is still pressed against the speaker.

"Don't touch that dial!"

This play is for Zoe Louisa, whose beautiful and brave
spirit is her father's inspiration.

Plus ça change, plus c'est la meme chose
Alphonse Karr

When things stop happening, they happen fast.
Peter Handke

MARGO VEIL
an entertainment

(A space that suggests a theater stage and some sort of broadcasting station. Bare except for a few tables and chairs. Perhaps there are microphones. A reel-to-reel tape deck somewhere.)

(In the distance, the dull thump of an explosion. And another. Dust drifts down from the ceiling. For a moment, the lights flicker. The performers enter one by one or in small groups, acknowledge each other and the audience, settle into places around the space. Another explosion, this one closer. A siren, and a dog howls somewhere. A NARRATOR *checks his watch. Someone flips on the reel-to-reel.)*

NARRATOR: It all began in a city that will remain nameless, on a night of thick suffocating fog. A young woman is hurrying homeward. She bumps into an odd figure, looming out of the fog...

(A WOMAN. *An* ODD MAN. *Soft sound of fog)*

WOMAN: I'm so sorry...

ODD MAN: Tell me, do you live here, in this city that will remain nameless?

WOMAN: Why, sure. Right on Lomas, near sixteenth.

ODD MAN: Do you know where Rudolph Morlock lives?

WOMAN: Why, no.

ODD MAN: Pity. Do you have a light? For my Tiparillo...

WOMAN: Why, yes. Here. *(Striking match)* I... Oooogh!

ODD MAN: What is it? What's the matter?

WOMAN: Nothing. I was just startled for a moment.

ODD MAN: Its my hands, isn't it? They frightened you.

WOMAN: No, no. Not at all.

ODD MAN: They disgusted you.

WOMAN: No, no, I...

ODD MAN: They disgusted you because they're not like other people's hands!

WOMAN: No. No!

ODD MAN: They're different.

WOMAN: Nooooooo!

ODD MAN: You think I'm a freak!

WOMAN: You're a complete nutburger!

ODD MAN: I'm not a nutburger, you hear me! I'll show you!! You bitch! You filthy little...

(The ODD MAN advances on the WOMAN, his hands outstretched toward her throat. She screams....)

NARRATOR: Enough. Yes, well.... Let's try something a little more...

(A girl, reading from Alice in Wonderland. As the GIRL READING ALICE tells the story, the NARRATOR talks to himself, makes notes about the significance of the tale.)

GIRL READING ALICE: The rabbit-hole went straight on like a tunnel for some way, and then dipped suddenly down, so suddenly Alice had not a moment to think about stopping herself before she was falling down what seemed to be a very deep well. Either the well was very deep, or she fell very slowly, for she had plenty of time as she went down to look about her. She looked at the sides of the well, and noticed they were filled with cupboards and bookshelves. She took a jar from one of the shelves as she passed; it was labeled "Orange Marmalade". Down, down, down. Would the fall never come to an end? There was nothing else to do, so Alice began talking.

ALICE: Dinah, my dear! I wish you were down here with me.

GIRL READING ALICE: Dinah was the cat.

ALICE: There are no mice in the air, I'm afraid, but you might catch a bat, and that's very like a mouse, you know. But do cats eat bats, I wonder?

GIRL READING ALICE: Alice went on, saying to herself in a dreamy sort of way...

Alice: Do cats eat bats? Do cats eat bats?

GIRL READING ALICE: And sometimes...

ALICE: Do bats eat cats?

GIRL READING ALICE: For you see, as she couldn't answer either question, it didn't much matter which way she put it.

NARRATOR: *(To himself, taking notes, under the reading from* Alice*)* Hmmm...yes...ah, gravity inversion, the physics of...orange marmalade, of course...ah! Ah! It's so obvious. Mothman prophecy and the...alchemical rabbit...the fall, fall from grace...into the...no...dark night of the soul....

ANNOUNCER: MARGO VEIL. An entertainment.

(MARGO VEIL appears.)

NARRATOR: Isn't it curious, Margo Veil? The city that only a few short months ago held so much promise— now seems cold, empty, frightening.

MARGO: Big apple, my ass.

NARRATOR: You came to this metropolis to be an actress, and within a week, you got a part.

MARGO: The lead.

NARRATOR: The show, *A Distant Candelabra* by the innovative playwright Arthur Vine, opened one night and closed the next. With its closing went your dreams of a successful acting career.

MARGO: I'll say. The papers called me attractive, but wooden. Wooden. They didn't even pay me for the last week's rehearsal. In fact, those bastards...

(HY HEPSTEIN's *shabby office.* HEPSTEIN, *Broadway show posters, a desk.*)

NARRATOR: And now, climbing the stairs to the office of Hiram Hepstein, your second-rate theatrical agent, you only hope you can talk the little man out of a loan so you won't have to write your parents for return railroad fare.

HEPSTEIN: Second-rate? Who got Ben Affleck a million and a half for that apocalypse thing? You don't know shit about the business. One phone call from me, that's all it takes. I handle LeStrange, I handle Winona, Sally Struthers. I convinced her to do the nude bit in that picture...

NARRATOR: Hy Hepstein seems to anticipate the purpose of your visit. Before you have the chance to sit down, he makes things coldly clear.

HEPSTEIN: Honey, this is a talent agency, not the loan department. You're down on your luck, but something'll turn up.

MARGO: No, Hy, this life isn't for me. My parents were right.

HEPSTEIN: Parents? I thought girls like you, they grew them in a vat in Minnesota.

MARGO: They said go to New York, Margo, give it a try, get it out of your system. *(Beat)* Well, I tried.

HEPSTEIN: I guess you have. You know, I went to see *A Distant Candelabra*. It stunk. You stunk in it. Who wrote that thing?

MARGO: Arthur Vine's his name.

HEPSTEIN: Handsome?

MARGO: Some of the girls thought so...

HEPSTEIN: Artistic? Deep?

MARGO: Some of the girls were really into his depth...

HEPSTEIN: You sleep with him?

MARGO: I...I...

HEPSTEIN: Forget it, honey. We're all young and stupid once.

(An uncomfortable silence)

MARGO: What's that odd statue on your desk, Hy? I never noticed it before.

HEPSTEIN: Just a piece of tourist junk my wife bought years ago. Near the Baltic Sea. Decorate your office, she said.

MARGO: Looks like an owl.

HEPSTEIN: Yeah. Maybe it does. *(Beat)* Look, sweetheart, if you're serious about going home, I got a way you can get there, and pick up a few bucks besides. Come to think of it, you'll even get a new dress out of the deal.

MARGO: Fairy Godmother Hy! Keep talking.

HEPSTEIN: An unusual setup. Nobody in the family wants to take the time, or maybe they're not interested. Hearts of stone.

MARGO: Come on, what's the job?

HEPSTEIN: It's an—acting job. You play the role of the grieving relative.

MARGO: What?

HEPSTEIN: Look, honey, you wanna get home? There's really nothing to this. You get train fare and five hundred dollars. Seems the railroad doesn't allow dead bodies to travel unaccompanied. You ride with the coffin to a town called, uh, Rapid City.

MARGO: Rapid City! That's only a hundred miles from Colby, my hometown.

HEPSTEIN: What a coincidence. You take the train from Grand Central, they put the coffin in the baggage car at Scranton, you sign for it, escort it to Rapid City. You want the job?

MARGO: Of course I do.

(HEPSTEIN *hands her a ticket.*)

HEPSTEIN: Here's your train ticket. You'll get the money in Rapid City at the Feldman Mortuary. The anonymous party paying for all this will leave an envelope for you with the mortuary manager.

MARGO: Five hundred dollars?

HEPSTEIN: Yep.

MARGO: Hy, I love you.

HEPSTEIN: I love you too. When you get home, don't forget to mail me my ten percent.

MARGO: What about the new dress?

HEPSTEIN: Already paid for. You get to pick it out at some store on Fifth—Valentino.

MARGO: Valentino. Well, get me. At least I'm going home in style.

HEPSTEIN: Don't get too stylish, sweetheart. You better make that dress— black.

(MARGO *steps behind a folding screen, changing clothes. Old outfit flies over the screen.*)

HEPSTEIN: *(On phone)* Louise, get me Sally Struthers, and a chicken salad on rye, heavy on the mayo...

NARRATOR: It's a strange role to play, isn't it, Margo? And yet you don't mind. You even get a thrill out of selecting the dress. It's been so long since you bought one.

(MARGO *steps from behind the screen in a smart little black dress.* HEPSTEIN'*s gone. A* CONDUCTOR. *A train*)

CONDUCTOR: All aboard!

(MARGO *takes a seat and the train takes off.*)

NARRATOR: As you roll pleasantly across New Jersey, any misgivings you had about your "acting job" drift away. But when the train stops at Scranton you find the station enveloped in a damp ominous fog.

(*The* BAGGAGE MASTER *appears.*)

NARRATOR: You introduce yourself to the baggage master.

MARGO: Hi. I'm Margo Veil.

NARRATOR: Then you catch sight of the coffin, and a strange feeling of dread comes over you.

BAGGAGE MASTER: *(Looking through some papers)* Margo Veil? You a relative?

MARGO: Of course. I'm a second cousin.

BAGGAGE MASTER: Sign here, please. And here. And here. And here.

(MARGO *does all the signing.*)

BAGGAGE MASTER: Rather unpleasant duty for a pretty young girl.

MARGO: I don't mind.

BAGGAGE MASTER: Escorting a rotting corpse, worms in the skull. Nasty night too. All this fog.

MARGO: I don't mind. It's not foggy inside the train.

BAGGAGE MASTER: Oh isn't it the truth. Moving world of its own. You're a bright little thing, aren't you? Step into the Baggage Office and I'll show you a model I've made of this very station, out of popsicle sticks...

(The BAGGAGE MASTER *grabs* MARGO. *A train whistle)*

MARGO: Gotta go.

*(*MARGO *pulls away. Another train whistle and she's on board. The* BAGGAGE MASTER *waves goodbye.)*

NARRATOR: The train is underway again, and its like the baggage master said. Isn't it, Margo? A moving world of its own, and you feel safe, secure. You put your head back against the seat cushion and...

(Beat, as MARGO *dozes off, snoring)*

NARRATOR: Margo! Margo Veil! What's that in your bag?

*(*MARGO *wakes, reaches into her bag, takes out the odd statue from* HEPSTEIN's *office.)*

MARGO: How the hell did this owl get...

*(*PROFESSOR HELEN AHRIMAN *stops by* MARGO's *seat.)*

AHRIMAN: That's not an owl. It's a striated marble carving of a Lithuanian demon, from long before the Christian era. A spirit of change. Very well preserved. Except for the tail.

MARGO: Tail?

AHRIMAN: That demon should have a tail. Broken off by tomb robbers, no doubt. I'm Professor Helen Ahriman. Archeology. Dead worlds. And you are...?

MARGO: Margo Veil.

AHRIMAN: Well Miss Veil, you're fortunate to possess such a singular artifact.

MARGO: Professor, does this demon have a name?

AHRIMAN: Of course, but no one knows it. Please, call me Helen. I'm on my way to the club car for a scotch and soda. You're welcome to...

MARGO: No thanks, Professor. (*Off she goes. On her way out...*)

AHRIMAN: (*Under her breath*) Little bitch...just like that other tease in my seminar....

NARRATOR: You drop off again to sleep.... You dream of an ancient city, ziggurats, obelisks, a grove of sacred trees. Its night in this city, a city undreamed of by archeologists. An owl-like demon, its wings spread wide, hovers over a stone labyrinth.

MARGO: (*In her sleep*) Ziggurats...night...labyrinth

NARRATOR: Footsteps in the corridor. You're deep inside your dream, Margo, and they don't wake you.

AHRIMAN: Shhhhh. A little tramp like you doesn't deserve to have.... Ah! Got it, and I'm gone.

(AHRIMAN *is gone, with the "owl." The* CONDUCTOR *appears, shakes* MARGO.)

CONDUCTOR: Excuse me, Miss. You fell asleep. Next station stop is Rapid City. RAPID CITY!

(*The train stops.* MARGO *gets off, looks around.*)

NARRATOR: The fog is thicker than ever in Rapid City. Everything is dissolving in a cool wet smoke. The coffin is taken from the train, moved through the fog to a waiting hearse.

CONDUCTOR: 'BOARD! Goodbye, Miss Veil. Good luck, and remember what I told you.

MARGO: You didn't tell me anything. You just...

(Whistle, and the train pulls away. The MORTUARY MANAGER *appears on the platform.)*

NARRATOR: The train pulls out, leaving you alone with the mortuary manager.

MORTUARY MANAGER: Envelope? Oh yes, there was one. I'm sorry, miss, but I left it at the mortuary office. I'll mail it to you in the morning.

MARGO: Oh, no. I need to have it now. I'm leaving Rapid City as soon as I can catch a bus.

MORTUARY MANAGER: Very well, Miss. This way. You can ride out to the mortuary with me.

(They get in the hearse, and off they go.)

MORTUARY MANAGER: I have to drive slow, on account of the fog. *(Beat, then louder)* On account of the fog.

(This time, a soft fog sound begins.)

MORTUARY MANAGER: Bad night. Good for that fellow, though.

MARGO: Who?

MORTUARY MANAGER: An inmate escaped. It was on the radio. From Byrdcliff, the asylum up on the hill.

MARGO: Gives me the willies. People like that wandering around.

(They pull up. A neon sign reads "Feldman Funeral Home". They get out.)

MORTUARY MANAGER: Here we are. Feldman Funeral Home. Wait here, Miss. I'll get your envelope.

MARGO: Oh, my purse. I left it on the seat of the hearse. I'll get it.

MORTUARY MANAGER: Go ahead. I'm sure the corpse won't mind. Heh heh heh...

(He's gone. MARGO steps toward the hearse.)

NARRATOR: As you head back toward the dark panelled hearse you think you see a man rising up in the darkness, out of the coffin. He moves in what seems like slow motion, and you're frozen, like a rabbit in front of a snake. *(Beat)* By the way, it's like a fantastic dream, isn't it, Sherry?

MARGO: I'm not Sherry. I'm Margo Veil.

NARRATOR: You can't believe its really happening, Sherry. But it is.

(The INMATE appears out of the shadows.)

INMATE: Get in the hearse. You drive.

(They get in. Car engines, and off they go.)

INMATE: Turn west on Route 46.

(They drive. They don't speak until...)

MARGO: So, you're taking your medication, I hope...

INMATE: You mean these? *(He takes out a pill bottle, shakes it, tosses it out the window.)*

INMATE: What's that town up ahead, sweetheart?

MARGO: Colby.

(Music in the distance, lights.)

INMATE: Kind of lively for this time of night.

MARGO: Its Friday. Every Friday night at the Grange Hall, there's a dance.

INMATE: You seem to know a lot about Colby.

MARGO: Its my hometown. I grew up around here.

INMATE: So did I.

NARRATOR: This lunatic looks familiar, doesn't he, Margo? You know him...

INMATE: Make a right and pull over.

MARGO: What for?

INMATE: You like to dance?

MARGO: You're crazy, you know that?

INMATE: So I've been told.

(Music. Lights. The Grange Hall dance)

INMATE: Just a guy and his girl...

(A slow number. To Know Him Is To Love Him *by the Teddy Bears.)*

To know, know, know him,
Is to love, love, love him,
And I do, and I do, and I do....

*(*MARGO *and the* INMATE *join the dance, holding each other close.)*

NARRATOR: As the music plays the crazy light leaves his eyes. He seems to Margo Veil to become more and more like a boy she loved in high school. *(Beat)* He's crying.

MARGO: Why are you crying?

INMATE: Because you're so beautiful.

*(*KEEPERS *in white coats burst in.* KEEPER TWO *holds a syringe.)*

KEEPER ONE: There he is!

KEEPER TWO: Come here, crazy boy! This needle's full of your sleepy-time medicine!

INMATE: Leave us alone.

(They grab him, give him a shot, and back away. He collapses in MARGO's *arms. She holds him as the music plays on.)*

(The music screeches to a stop. Silence. The other dancers disappear. Suddenly MARGO *drops the inmate's body to the floor. The Colby dancehall,* MARGO, *and the inmate boy are gone.)*

NARRATOR: A bar in the Ramona Hotel, downtown Albuquerque, New Mexico.

(The bar, the NARRATOR *at a table alone. The* BARMAID *is on the phone.)*

BARMAID: *(Into phone)* I don't want you watching that Comedy Central shit, you hear me. You be in bed by eleven, O K? You got school tomorrow. And I don't want you playing air guitar.... Then play, dammit, but not while you jump up and down on your bed like a crazy person. That bed is damn near new....

(A girl's laughter from the other end of the line.)

BARMAID: Who's that I hear laughing back there? Zat Yvette? It is, isn't it? Just put her on the goddamn phone....

YVETTE: *(Laughing) Hola?*

BARMAID: Miss Yvette Chavez, you know damn well you're not allowed in my house. And keep your hands off my son. He's just fourteen, and he's a good kid. I don't want him ending up like your brothers, doing five to ten in Las Lunas. You just get outta my house. Put your little panties on and get the hell outta there now, or I'm calling the cops, let them haul your ass out. Won't be the first time, will it, Miss Chavez? Put my son back on the phone... Yeah...Yeah, I did. Damn right

I did. Look, I'll be home in about two hours, and I wanna find you sleeping. You got school tomorrow... Yeah. Yeah, you know I will.

(From a distance, applause)

BARMAID: *(Into phone)* Show's over. Gotta go, love you. Bye.

(MARGO enters, sits at a table. The BARMAID comes over.)

BARMAID: Good show tonight, Miss Veil?

MARGO: Good as this piece of crap gets, I guess. I don't know anymore. Pretzels, please. And a vodka gimlet.

(The BARMAID goes to get her drink.)

NARRATOR: You never thought *A Distant Candelabra* would tour, did you Margo? Twenty cities in two months. They called you, but not for the leading role.

MARGO: I'm the ghost of the mother—no lines— and one of the spirits in the dream sequence. I wail. Aaaah-oooooooo!

(The BARMAID sets down MARGO's drink.)

MARGO: Two more nights in Albuquerque. You actually live here?

BARMAID: Right on Lomas, near sixteenth.

MARGO: Overgrown cowtown. They put us in the El Rancho down on Central. Old woman in the next room keeps talking to someone who's not there. "You gonna burn in hell, Bobby. Your pretty face is gonna melt right off your fucking skull..."

BARMAID: Listen, Miss Veil, I know its none of my business, but you don't seem all that happy.

MARGO: I'll say.

BARMAID: You might want to see Bo.

MARGO: Bo?

BARMAID: Bo Diddley. The RnB singer? He lives here, got a ranch in the South Valley. He's retired, and now he talks to people all the time. Bo knows.

MARGO: Bo knows what?

BARMAID: Just go out and see him, O K? You can't miss it. The house has a gold record nailed to the front door. Oh yeah. Some guy was looking for you during the show...

(ARTHUR VINE *appears, good looking in a writerly way.*)

BARMAID: That's him.

(*The* BARMAID *goes back behind the bar as* VINE *sits at* MARGO's *table.*)

NARRATOR: Arthur Vine. A shiver goes up your spine, doesn't it, Margo? A little frisson. Is that love? You should be angry, Margo Veil. He didn't call. Not once.

MARGO: What are you doing here, Arthur?

VINE: Checking on my play. Margo, you're wonderful in it.

MARGO: No I'm not. And you didn't even watch it.

VINE: I couldn't get here in time. I was glued to the porn channel in my room. Right upstairs. 802. Why don't we go up and...

MARGO: You know, you're a son of a bitch. Sleeping with you, Arthur, it's like being with...nobody. You're not even there. You're an emotional pygmy. You...

VINE: I love you, Margo.

MARGO: No, you don't. And your stupid play is...

NARRATOR: Talking of this and that, Margo Veil and Arthur Vine are interrupted by the appearance of a fat man in a bad suit...

(The fat man, MISTER RONCALLON, *rushes over to their table.)*

RONCALLON: Good evening, Miss Veil. My name's Roncallon. Milo Roncallon. I'm a particular fan of your show. I've seen it twenty-three times, in six cities. Toledo, Chicago, Dubuque, Cincinnati, Toledo...

MARGO: Get a life.

RONCALLON: I've been dying to meet the author. You're Arthur Vine?

VINE: As a matter of fact, I...

RONCALLON: I've got a message for you. From Rhonda.

VINE: My ex—

RONCALLON: She's Rhonda Roncallon now, Mister Vine. We're living off your life insurance, and it would be embarrassing if you climbed up out of the grave. Resurfaced. An inconsistency in the fabric of space-time, with economic...

*(*RHONDA *appears.)*

RHONDA: Stop talking. Just kill the fuck. Do it, Herbert!

RONCALLON: Herbert? Rhonda, my name's....

*(*RONCALLON, *or Herbert, leaps at* VINE. *They struggle.* RONCALLON *has his hands around* VINE's *throat, and* VINE *is twitching, turning blue.)*

VINE: Margo!

*(*MARGO *grabs a steak knife from a table, stabs* RONCALLON *in the back.* RONCALLON *collapses, groans, lies still.*

MARGO: Oh, shit. Mister Roncallon...he's dead.

VINE: Yeah. He is.

MARGO: You don't seem too upset about it.

VINE: I'm not his mother.

(The BARMAID *reaches for the phone.)*

BARMAID: *(On phone)* Officer, I want to report this girl who broke into my house. Yvette Chavez. You know that Chavez family, has that funky house near the auto-salvage on Lagunitas, growing pot in their backyard....

NARRATOR: The barmaid's calling Bo Diddley. Or the police. You don't know which, do you Margo?

*(*VINE *checks out the corpse with the knife in its back, the* BARMAID *on the phone.)*

VINE: Do you know what time it is, Margo?

MARGO: I...I..

VINE: Time to jump.

(Interstate 40. VINE *and* MARGO *in a car, doing eighty.)*

NARRATOR: I-40 heading west out of Albuquerque toward Gallup, New Mexico. Past Grants, past Bibo, past Tuba City, under a black sky. The radio plays...

COMPANY: *(Song on radio, sung)*
Jesus is on that mainline,
Tell him what you want,
Jesus is on that mainline,
Tell him what you want,
Jesus is on that mainline,
Tell him what you want,
You can call him up and tell him what you want
The line ain't never busy,
Tell him what you want,
The line ain't never busy,
Tell him what you want...

(Jesus is on the Mainline *continues softly as a preacher,*
REVEREND FORD, *speaks over it...*

REVEREND FORD: This is the Reverend Cletus Ford welcoming you to W K N M, the radio manger of the

baby Jesus. Are you lost? Troubled? Do you find
yourself riding in shiny automobiles with people
got the morals of a squid? Destination unknown...
What's a human being made of? Salt water out of the
sea, handful of dust from the garden, and a thimbleful
of breath from the East Wind. He will live awhile, and
then go into the darkness where the worm never dies.

MARGO: Where we going?

REVEREND FORD: Faith is blind, but she's long-legged,
with big....

VINE: Ah! Our exit!

(The radio suddenly goes dead.)

NARRATOR: And Vine pulls off into the parking lot of
the Giant Truck Stop, weaves his little Honda between
the eighteen wheelers till he's near a long pre-fab shed.

*(A neon sign lights up: TANNING SALON AND
STYLING ACADEMY. VINE knocks. MARGO looks
at the sign.)*

MARGO: Tanning Salon and Styling Academy. Who
knew that truckers took an interest in...

VINE: It's a Translation Parlor. *(He knocks again.)*

MARGO: Like from English to....Lithuanian?

VINE: Shhh. Translation is illegal.

*(VINE knocks again. In another area [within] BIG BETTY and
her stepson DWAYNE appear. BIG BETTY sits in a large chair
with a pint of Night Train. She sings Let it Shine on Me to
herself. DWAYNE's shirt is open to the navel. Somewhere,
a Translation Machine behind curtains. Knocking)*

BIG BETTY: We're closed.

DWAYNE: *(Shouting)* Closed!

(More knocking)

BIG BETTY: Fuck you! I'm takin' my medicine.

DWAYNE: *(Shouting)* Medicine!

(BIG BETTY *sips her Night Train.*)

VINE: Betty! This is Arthur Vine!

BIG BETTY: Really? What are you this time?

VINE: About 5'11'. Artistic.

BIG BETTY: Are you attractive? In any special sense?

VINE: Attractive? I'm desperate.

BIG BETTY: My heart. It bleeds. Dwayne, let the bastard in.

(DWAYNE *ushers* VINE *and* MARGO *in.*)

BIG BETTY: Good evening. I'm Betty, and this is my stepson Dwayne. Even after hours, we try to accommodate...to serve the needy..to..

VINE: I need a jump. Two of them. I've brought along a compliant and mildly retarded young woman.

MARGO: What?

VINE: An actorette. The police may be here at any moment. She just killed someone.

BIG BETTY: All by herself, Arthur? I have no desire to jump you and then see you arrested.

VINE: My worry. This shell I'm in is riddled with cancer. Terminal. Two weeks, a month at the outside...

DWAYNE: The two of you want a simple switch?

VINE: Dwayne, you disgust me. As usual. You know I don't do cross-sexual.

BIG BETTY: *(To* MARGO*)* We're a respectable establishment, darling, though the authorities have forced Translation Parlors like mine to operate outside the law. You think I wouldn't rather be in a goddamn stripmall?

MARGO: I...I...

BIG BETTY: We do accurate body transfer between consenting parties. No one will ever find you. If they do, it won't be you. Just the shell, with someone else looking out of your eyes. *(Beat)* You'll have all the skills and memories of your new shell, and somewhere deep inside, you'll still have yourself. Your soul, if I may use that metaphysical term, is transferred. It's hard to notice, the soul—but its there, like a shadow in your new mind. *(Beat)* Sometimes the client has an idea. A movie star, someone he saw in a poolhall. I'm interested in these ideas. I do my best to make them a reality, to...

VINE: There's no time for all this shit.

BIG BETTY: What's her name, Arthur?

VINE: Vivian. Vivian Clay.

BIG BETTY: It would be easier for me to help you, Vivian Clay, if you were not too concerned with issues of...physical ability.

MARGO: I guess. I don't want to spend my life in jail. My parents would be..

DWAYNE: Shut up.

BIG BETTY: Dwayne can be so rude. *(Beat)* We have desperate clients. Some are in the holding pen out back. Others sit impatiently by the telephone. Some are in criminal situations like yourselves. Others are ill. Others are unspeakably ugly, others are dissatisfied with...

VINE: Let's do it.

BIG BETTY: *(Laughs)* You're addicted, Arthur. You know that, don't you? To the jump. Each body grows uncomfortable after a few months. Itches.

(DWAYNE *laughs.*)

BIG BETTY: How many in back, Dwayne?

DWAYNE: Two. Man and a woman.

BIG BETTY: Perfect.

DWAYNE: She's hot. Tsss!

BIG BETTY: Spare us your opinions. *(To* MARGO *and* VINE*)* You won't get to see your new shell until you look in a mirror.

DWAYNE: Follow me.

BIG BETTY: Follow Dwayne. Relax. It's painless. A technician will be with you shortly. It's all very technical back there. You need to be a college graduate to know what the fuck goes on. I'm only administration. Dwayne, help her strip.

(DWAYNE *leads* MARGO *behind a curtain of the Translation Machine.*)

VINE: How do I find you again, if I...

BIG BETTY: I'll be there when you need me, Arthur. I'm always around.

(VINE *goes behind another curtain of the Translation Machine.* DWAYNE *reappears.* BIG BETTY *sips her Night Train. Strange sound of the body-swapping translation device. The lights flicker, then come back up.*)

(*From behind* MARGO's *curtain steps* RUTA, *a young Lithuanian girl, very beautiful. She paws at the air. A rope is tied to her wrist. A Lithuanian peasant, her* GRANDFATHER, *appears and takes the end of the rope.*)

RUTA: Oh my God! I'm blind...

GRANDFATHER: Skambutis. Come, Ruta, the cows need milking.

(He leads her offstage.)

(From behind VINE's *curtain steps a sophisticated older actor,* EDGAR LESTRANGE. *Moustache, tuxedo. A girl with a clipboard,* YVETTE, *appears.)*

YVETTE: Places, Mister LeStrange.

LESTRANGE: Thank you, Yvette.

*(*LESTRANGE *is gone.* BIG BETTY *is gone. The Translation Parlor is gone.* DWAYNE *and* YVETTE *remain.* YVETTE *chews gum, blows huge bubbles, pops them.* DWAYNE *plays air guitar with great energy, and sings.)*

DWAYNE: *(Sings)* Bo Diddley's a gunslinger,
Bo Diddley's a gunslinger, yeahhh
I got a story I really wanna tell,
About Bo Diddley at the O K Corral
Bo Diddley didn't stand no mess,
Wore a gun on his hip
And a rose on his chest
Bo Diddley's a gunslinger
Bo Diddley's a gunslinger, yeahhh,
Must be!

YVETTE: Must be!

DWAYNE: Sho' 'nuff!

YVETTE: Sho' 'nuff!

*(*DWAYNE *and* YVETTE *are gone. A Broadway stage, with audience.)*

NARRATOR: *(In audience)* A Broadway stage. On it, Edgar LeStrange, in the role of Rudolph Morlock.

LESTRANGE: *(Playing Rudolph Morlock)* Step out here on the terrace, Nikki, where we can be alone.

NIKKI: A full moon, Rudolph! How lovely.
Look, Rudolph! The lights of Louisville! That steamboat
drifting by on the Ohio...how lovely!

LESTRANGE: Shut up, Nikki. Your bubble-headed
platitudes drive me crazy.

NIKKI: Don't give me shit, Rudolph. Not when
Louisville is so beautiful. Not on New Year's Eve. We
promised each other a new start in the new year.
Remember?

LESTRANGE: Of course I remember, darling. Have some
champagne. (*He pours her a glass, then raises his own
empty one.*) To us!

NIKKI: To us! (*She drains her glass of champagne*) Let's go
in. It's chilly out here on the terrace.

LESTRANGE: We can't, Nikki darling. Not yet.

NIKKI: Why not?

LESTRANGE: I need to tell you something. Nikki,
you remember the last mayor of Louisville?

NIKKI: Poor man. Poisoned, then drowned in his
bathtub.

LESTRANGE: And the Chief Judge of the Criminal Court?

NIKKI: Poisoned at a party. They say the punch was...

LESTRANGE: And a local prostitute. Darlene her name
was. Found face down in the goldfish pond near my
garden pavilion?

NIKKI: (*Feeling the poison*) Hold me, Rudolph. I feel
dizzy, weak...

LESTRANGE: That's because I poisoned your
champagne. You'll die like all the others. And now,
off the terrace with you!

(*He picks up her body, throws her off the terrace.*)

NIKKI: *(Falling and fading)* Ah! Ahhhhhhhhhhh.....

(A THUNK, then silence. LESTRANGE [as Morlock] looks down from the terrace.)

LESTRANGE: Happy New Year, Nikki darling. From the Louisville Poisoner.

(He laughs maniacally. The police rush in!)

CAPTAIN: Rudolph Morlock, you're under arrest.

(LESTRANGE rushes to the edge of the terrace.)

LESTRANGE: You're too late, Captain.

CAPTAIN: Morlock! Get away from there! No!

(LESTRANGE leaps off the terrace into the abyss.)

LESTRANGE: Tooooooooo laaaaate....

(And a THUNK. Wild applause. NIKKI and the CAPTAIN take a bow. The audience is thrilled. LESTRANGE takes a bow. Renewed applause.)

(The terrace is gone, and the COMPANY MANAGER appears, backstage.)

LESTRANGE: I'm telling you, Charles. It's been five years. I can't be Rudolph Morlock for even one more night. If I do this show again, I'll...

COMPANY MANAGER: It's only a play, Edgar.

LESTRANGE: To an actor, a superb actor, its never entirely make believe.

COMPANY MANAGER: I can't release you from your contract. Besides, Edgar LeStrange is The Louisville Poisoner. The audience loves you. We're selling out every...

LESTRANGE: If I poison one more human being, I'll lose my mind.

COMPANY MANAGER: Go home, Edgar. Think it over. If its a matter of salary...

LESTRANGE: You haven't understood a word I've said. I quit!

COMPANY MANAGER: I'll sue you for everything you...

LESTRANGE: Fuck yourself, Charles.

(LESTRANGE *heads for the stagedoor. A* NARRATOR. *Outside the theater, an* AUTOGRAPH SEEKER *and a* TAXI DRIVER.)

NARRATOR: You slam the stagedoor shut behind you.

LESTRANGE: *(To himself)* Maybe a rep company in the midlands...Lear! Blow winds, crack your cheeks! Howl hurricanoes...

AUTOGRAPH SEEKER: For my wife. She's... *(Suddenly the* AUTOGRAPH SEEKER *looks up.)* That statue is...WATCH OUT!

(LESTRANGE, *hit by a falling piece of statuary, clutches his head, then crumples to the ground, moaning.)*

NARRATOR: Fate's a funny thing. Isn't it, Edgar LeStrange? Or is it Arthur Vine? One moment you're onstage, applause ringing in your ears. An odd little gargoyle topples from a roof cornice and the next moment you're lying in the gutter, blood oozing from your head, and you can't remember who you are. Not a clue.

(LESTRANGE *sits up, holding his head. He fumbles for his wallet.)*

LESTRANGE: Ah! My wallet. Perhaps a driver's license will...

NARRATOR: You left your wallet backstage, didn't you? No I D, just some folding money in your pants pocket.

(*A* TAXI DRIVER *leans over* LESTRANGE.)

TAXI DRIVER: Hey! Hey, Mister! That chunk of stone hit you right in the head. You alright?

LESTRANGE: I think so. I....

TAXI DRIVER: You need to get home. My cab's just...

LESTRANGE: I need to get away from these streets, these theaters, these lights... There must be a train station...

TAXI DRIVER: Grand Central?

LESTRANGE: Grand Central. That's it. Take me there.

(A train station, a TRAIN CLERK*)*

NARRATOR: And in a few minutes you're on a ticket line, with no idea where you're going. Your turn. Step up to the window.

TRAIN CLERK: Where to?

LESTRANGE: I'm not sure. My head is still...

TRAIN CLERK: You got a line behind you. Make up your mind.

LOUD SPEAKER: Southern Flyer to Pittsburg, Columbus, Louisville, Memphis, New Orleans, now boarding on Track 7.

LESTRANGE: What was that?

LOUD SPEAKER: Pittsburg, Columbus, Louisville, Louisville, Louisville...

LESTRANGE: One way...to Louisville!

(Train whistle. A train. The same CONDUCTOR *as before)*

CONDUCTOR: 'Board! Moving world of its own! 'Board!

*(*LESTRANGE *boards.)*

NARRATOR: Ah, the observation car. Why not sit next to that attractive woman by the window, strike up a conversation. Perhaps something will remind you of who you are...

(LeStrange *sits next to* Roxanne.)

Narrator: By the way, her name's Roxanne. She's a student at the University of Kentucky.

Roxanne: Art history. I'm into Flemish painting. All those little demons. There's one with five legs, tin funnel for a hat, and his face up his own ass.

LeStrange: Yes, well, I...

Roxanne: Don't I know you?

LeStrange: Do you now?

Roxanne: Yes. Yes! You're that actor, Edgar LeStrange. You were in that movie in the eighties, *Feast of Blood.*

LeStrange: Sorry, darling. I'm not...

Roxanne: You chained that girl in the cellar, had your pet monkeys rip her clothes off, and poisoned her.

LeStrange: Poisoned? Did you say...

Roxanne: 'Scuse me?

LeStrange: Ah! Ah! *(Beat)* I neglected to introduce myself. My name is Rudolph Morlock.

Roxanne: I get it. You celebs like to travel incognito. I won't say a word to anyone in Louisville.

LeStrange: Louisville! That's exactly where I'm going.

Roxanne: Me, too. My uncle lives there.

LeStrange: What a coincidence.

(A long silence between them)

Roxanne: You know, Mister Morlock, this world we live in...

LeStrange: Yes?

Roxanne: Look out there.

LeStrange: It's night-time. I can't see anything.

ROXANNE: I can. Strip mall with a laundromat, Dunkin'
Donuts, tropical fish store, tank glows in the window,
one huge angelfish gliding alone and slow in the green
light. Turn and turn again under the cold stars...
A vacant lot overrun by weeds, plastic trash bags torn
open and my baby brother squats by a fire, stupid
spider tattoo on his left cheek, blood under his
fingernails, dirty piece of string knotted around
his neck....
There's the Riverside Motel, naked people on the
sagging beds, full of guilt and fear, fucking away their
troubles in the dawn's early light. Tractor-trailer out
of Memphis hauling chicken parts, driver with a tin
funnel on his head doing ninety down the river road
on a twelve percent grade. High beams on, white light
bursts through the motel rooms one by one, lighting
the pale bodies like a photoflash. In the motel office
doorway a man in a Santa Claus suit is sitting on a
milkcrate. "What you want for Christmas, little girl?"

LESTRANGE: It's still July. Christmas is six mo...

ROXANNE: I'm visiting my mother. She's in a home,
somefuck suburb of Louisville. Highland Park. She
doesn't even know who the fuck I am. There's this
party at my uncle's house. You wanna go?

LESTRANGE: I'd be delighted. You know, Roxanne,
I hate certain people enormously. My wife Nikki. My
ex- wife....Rhonda, I believe. The judge who sentenced
me to seven years in prison for a harmless peccadillo.
And all his cronies.

ROXANNE: My uncle's a judge.

LESTRANGE: What a coincidence.

ROXANNE: What's a peccadillo?

LESTRANGE: I was a chemical researcher for Feldman
Pharmaceuticals. During the company picnic some girls

from the steno pool mistakenly inhaled a powerful euphoric and ran naked among the trees. Stripping off my labcoat, I followed and...

NARRATOR: And so, talking of this and that, they arrived in

CONDUCTOR: LOUISVILLE! LOUISVILLE! Ten minutes!

(A party. Hideous laughter. Drinks. ROXANNE, LESTRANGE, *the* JUDGE, CRONIES. *Music)*

LESTRANGE: Allow me to make the punch.

JUDGE: Excellent!

*(*LESTRANGE *makes punch in a large punchbowl, tasting, adding ingredients.)*

LESTRANGE: A number ten can of pineapple juice, quart of Jim Beam, dollop of peppermint schnapps, dash of bitters, a tablespoon of my secret ingredient. And a pint of Night Train.

(As LESTRANGE *pours in the Night Train, the* JUDGE *and four of his* CRONIES *come forward in a tight group.)*

JUDGE: Excellent. I sentenced that jump addict to thirty years. Hung him out to...

CRONY ONE: A slap on the wrist, Judge. Time, crime, time, crime.

CRONY TWO: Turn all of Louisville into a state correctional facility!

CRONY THREE: Cattle prods, Mister Roncallon. Compulsory prayer meetings.

CRONY FOUR: Let's sterilize them all!

(The JUDGE *and his* CRONIES *repeat their lines twice more, in an overlapping round, getting louder. When they finish, they laugh maniacally until...)*

JUDGE: Shut up!

(The CRONIES *are silent, and the music stops.)*

LeStrange: Has everyone had some punch?

ALL: *(Except* ROXANNE*)* Yes!

LeStrange: Delicious, isn't it?

(Wild music. Ernie Fields' Tuxedo Junction. *All dance. As they dance, they collapse one by one, crash to the floor, and die. The* JUDGE *falls into the punchbowl.* LeStrange *and* ROXANNE *keep dancing. A* NARRATOR *rises up from among the dead.)*

NARRATOR: Suddenly, the doorbell rings.

(The music stops. DING! DING! There's a small dapper man in a suit, MORTMAIN. ROXANNE *lets him in. He has an Eastern European accent.)*

MORTMAIN: I am Mortmain the Magician. I was hired to perform at this festivity.

ROXANNE: Well, you might as well come in.

MORTMAIN: Just close-up stuff you understand. With what you're paying me, a large illusion was out of the question. *(He looks around.)* Everyone is dead. They won't be amused by the color-changing silks.

ROXANNE: Stay awhile. Have a beer.

NARRATOR: *(Rising again from the dead)* At that moment, an odd owl-like statue tumbles from a high shelf.

LeStrange: Owwwww! My head... *(He falls to his knees, holding his head.)*

LeStrange: My God! I remember. I'm an actor. A superb actor. My name is Edgar LeStrange.

ROXANNE: Duh.

LeStrange: No...I'm a writer. Arthur...something. Rhonda, that bitch! *(He heads for the exit. On his way out...*

To himself) I need a jump...what a rogue and peasant slave am I, the bare bodkin of...

*(*MORTMAIN, ROXANNE, *and the corpses remain.)*

MORTMAIN: Allow me to clear away these corpses.

*(*MORTMAIN *snaps his fingers, and the corpses of the* JUDGE *and his* CRONIES *rise up and walk offstage.)*

MORTMAIN: I am Mortmain the Magician.

(A telephone begins to ring. Ring! Ring! [and continuing under...])

ROXANNE: You said that.

MORTMAIN: What?

ROXANNE: *(Imitating his accent)* I am Mortmain the Magician.

MORTMAIN: If you pick that up, it stops making that noise.

ROXANNE: Wise ass. *(She picks up the phone)* Hello?

*(*ROXANNE *listens briefly, then holds her hand over the phone, telling* MORTMAIN...)*

ROXANNE: It's my boyfriend. He's calling from Lithuania.

MORTMAIN: What a coincidence.

(In a separate Lithuanian space, ROXANNE'S BOYFRIEND *appears.)*

ROXANNE'S BOYFRIEND: *(On phone)* Roxanne, Jesus. What took you so damn long to answer the phone? I need to talk to you. You won't believe the shit I'm in here. I met Mister Secundas, turns out he's a fat guy in a bad suit and big moustache, picks me up at the airport in Vilnius, drives me to Kaunas telling dirty jokes in his lousy English all the way, and he checks me into this Hotel Palanga. I went out drinking that night—me,

him, his partners and three women look like cheap
Russian whores. They order some kind of local liquor,
and it hits me hard. Next thing I remember is I wake
up at dawn on the banks of this stinking river they got
here, the Nemanus, and two fishermen in a rowboat are
pointing at me and laughing. Somebody stole my pants.
The grass is wet, I'm soaked and shivering, my head
is pounding, and then I realize my wallet was in
those pants. And my room key. I got back to my hotel
wrapped in a blanket I stole off somebody's washline.
The room was stripped clean. My papers, passport,
money...I got nothing. Nothing. It's fucked. The deal
is fucked. It's my job. I'm gonna be fired.

ROXANNE: *(Softly, to herself)* Blue folder...

ROXANNE'S BOYFRIEND: Look, Roxanne, you gotta fax
me the papers on my desk, in the blue folder—

ROXANNE: Hotel Palanga, 802.

ROXANNE'S BOYFRIEND: Hotel Palanga, room 802,
Kaunas. And money. I need money. Send me ten
thousand dollars, in small bills. Western Union or
something. Roxanne, you gotta do this or I am
completely screwed. My balls are in the Lithuanian
fire here. You know, this whole place is nuts. Before we
go out last night, Secundas takes me into a church to
show me some statue, and these old ladies are in there
praying, and the priest comes out with a dead calf
draped over his shoulders, drops it on the altar. He's
saying something in this fucking language they got and
he tears at the calf with his bare hands, ripping it apart.
He ends up gnawing on a leg, blood all over his priestly
vestments and the old ladies just keep praying.

ROXANNE: *(Softly to herself)* Seven dwarfs...

ROXANNE'S BOYFRIEND: I swear these people worship
the fucking seven dwarfs. Or the goddamn trees. Hey,
Roxanne, I got you a present. At this street market. I'm

not gonna tell you what it is. I know you're gonna like
it.... Look, you fax me those papers in the blue folder,
and if everything goes O K, I'll be home by next
Thursday evening. We'll go out somewhere. A movie
or something. Roxanne, I love you. I gotta go.

(ROXANNE *hangs up the phone.*)

ROXANNE: What am I supposed to do? There's no blue
folder. He doesn't even have a desk. Or a job. I can't
help him every time he...

MORTMAIN: I am Mortmain the Magician.

ROXANNE: You said...

MORTMAIN: I am the true Mortmain the Magician.
Another man also calls himself Mortmain the Magician.
His real name is Cardano. He's performing this evening
at the Majestic here in Louisville. He even calls his
show Mortmain's Realm of Shadows.
Allow me tell you a story. I was travelling with a
small carnival through Leituva— Lithuania. We played
Ignalina, Vilnius, Trakai. Then we moved on, this time
to a vacant lot outside of Kaunas.

(ROXANNE *is gone.* MORTMAIN *sits at a small table.*)

MORTMAIN: The Nemanus ran right by our tents, still
beautiful and slow. Even forty years under the Russian
scum couldn't change the river. Every night the people
came to us out of their cramped apartments and their
pathetic farms, stinking of smoked fish, drawn like
moths to the light. We had a thrill wheel, donkey rides,
a haunted swing, a blood-sweating hippopotamus in a
cage.

HIPPO: *(O S)* Unnnhhh! Aaroogh!

MORTMAIN: One night...

(RUTA *and her* GRANDFATHER *appear, at a distance.*
He leads her on a rope. A PITCHMAN.)

PITCHMAN: Mortmain! He knows all! Sees all! The sealed book of the future is open before him. With the help of Jesu Christas he travels between the worlds. Ask him anything! He knows about love! Money! He knows the language of the bees!

(The GRANDFATHER *leads the sightless girl to* MORTMAIN.*)*

GRANDFATHER: This is my granddaughter Ruta. She's blind, but she heard the talk about you. She wants to know her future.

MORTMAIN: Give me your hand.

*(*MORTMAIN *takes her hand, studies her palm, then looks long into her face.)*

MORTMAIN: *(To audience)* She was so beautiful, so pure. How could I tell her the truth? What I saw in my mind. An empty and endless corridor in an anonymous office building, Ruta on her knees under the fluorescents, weeping. *(To* RUTA*)* You will marry a handsome and devoted husband who will love you more than his own life. The two of you will live long, full of joy. I see all this in the lines of your palm.

RUTA: Did you hear that, grandfather?

GRANDFATHER: Yes, Ruta. I heard it all.

RUTA: Thank you. Thank you so much.

*(*MORTMAIN *bends down and kisses her palm. Then, at last, he releases her hand.)*

GRANDFATHER: Come, my little bird. Let's go.

(Her GRANDFATHER *leads* RUTA *away.)*

MORTMAIN: That night I couldn't sleep. Her face never left me. I knew she would be my wife. I found the little farm they lived on. I brought gifts for Ruta and her grandfather—a pineapple, and a box of tea.

(The farm. RUTA *and her* GRANDFATHER. MORTMAIN
hands them the gifts.)

GRANDFATHER: Skambutis. Thank you.

RUTA: You are very kind.

MORTMAIN: Ruta, I know this will sound strange. I've
only known you for a very short time—but I want you
to marry me.

RUTA: *(Laughs gently)* I'm blind, Mister Mortmain the
Magician. I won't be a good wife. You'd need to lead
me everywhere, to...

MORTMAIN: I don't care. I love you. You can't spend
your life on this farm. Marry me, Ruta. I am a poor man
now, but I am working on my magic act. I will make
illusions no one has ever seen. We'll be rich. We'll live
like a king and his queen.

(He takes her in his arms.)

*(Wedding music. A strange Lithuanian wedding dance,
with* RUTA *and* MORTMAIN *dancing at its center.
The music and the dance end.)*

GUEST ONE: Many children!

GUEST TWO: Much happiness!

*(*CARDANO *appears at the wedding. He stands silently,
observing the festivities.)*

MORTMAIN: Who's that?

PITCHMAN: Cardano. A sort of clown. I hired him this
morning.

MORTMAIN: We're not a circus.

PITCHMAN: He does a show. Alone. Just him in a tent.
He came cheap.

MORTMAIN: What does he do?

PITCHMAN: Very funny man, Cardano. He imitates people in the audience. The voices, the walk, the gesturing. He's always someone else. He even imitates me while I was hiring him. I couldn't tell who was me—him or me!

(The PITCHMAN *waves to* CARDANO, *and* CARDANO *waves back with an identical gesture.)*

PITCHMAN: He's fluent in Lithuanian, English... but I think he's Italian.

MORTMAIN: Signore Cardano, welcome to my wedding!

CARDANO: *(Imitating him exactly)* Congratulations, Mortmain. Laba diena! You have a most beautiful wife!

MORTMAIN: Thank you.

CARDANO: *(Imitating Mortmain)* Thank you.

MORTMAIN: And on we travelled, our little show.

CARDANO: Our little show...

*(*RUTA *is alone in the countryside. A stork pecks the dirt nearby. She sings a sad and passionate song.)*

RUTA: *(Sings to herself)* Lume, lume, schwester welt
Ich werdas genug habenas welt... Lume, lume...
Wenn ich kein brot pilius gatve
Und auch keinas kava balta
Welt, lume, lume.....

*(*CARDANO *listens in. He's wearing some clothes of* MORTMAIN's. *He applauds.)*

RUTA: Is that you, Mortmain? I thought you were working on the drowning man trick until dinner time.

CARDANO: *(In* MORTMAIN's *voice)* I couldn't wait to be with you.

*(*RUTA *smiles, stands, holds open her arms.)*

CARDANO: (MORTMAIN's *voice*) Don't touch me. I'm filthy, from the workshop—oil and paint.

(RUTA *is fooled.* CARDANO *caresses her face, her lips. His hands circle her waist. Suddenly he pulls her to him. Her hands come up to touch his face. She screams, shoves him away.*)

RUTA: Who are you? I felt your face. You're not Mortmain...
Is Mortmain dead?

(CARDANO *laughs. He no longer imitates* MORTMAIN, *and his accent is Italian.*)

CARDANO: (*In his own voice*) I wish he were. My name is Cardano. I stole his clothes, I...

RUTA: Get out of here. Before he returns.

CARDANO: No, bellissima.

RUTA: You must!

CARDANO: I can't go. I love you.

RUTA: No one else can love me. I'm Mortmain's wife.

CARDANO: You can't see the ugliness of the world. It can't hurt you, can't touch you. You're an angel on...

(MORTMAIN *enters.*)

MORTMAIN: Cardano! What are you doing here?

(RUTA *runs to* MORTMAIN, *hides behind him.*)

CARDANO: I tried to make love to your wife. I didn't succeed. My face. It gave me away.

MORTMAIN: If I see you with Ruta again, Cardano, I will kill you. I swear it on my mother's grave.

(*He advances on* CARDANO. CARDANO *backs away.*)

CARDANO: Don't hurt me, Mortmain. After all, I'm just like you. *(To* RUTA*)* I won't forget you, bellissima. Not ever!

(He's gone, and MORTMAIN *takes* RUTA *in his arms.)*

(The countryside is gone and they're in a backstage dressing room. MORTMAIN *prepares to perform. A* FRENCH STAGE MANAGER *appears.)*

FRENCH STAGE MANAGER: M'sieu Mortmain. Cinq minutes.

*(*MORTMAIN *follows the* FRENCH STAGE MANAGER *off.* RUTA *alone)*

RUTA: Three years later, we were in Paris. My husband is a genius. His illusions took us far from that shabby carnival, that blood- sweating hippopotamus.

HIPPO: *(O S)* Unnnnhhh! Arooogh!

RUTA: To Warsaw, Cracow, Budapest, and then to this theatre of the Cirque D'Hiver where Mortmain's Realm of Shadows has already played three months! Best of all, he taught me to assist him. I even go out onstage, and hand him his saw.

(Applause)

RUTA: Hear that? He'll meet me back here after he takes his bows. We're meeting friends at Les Trois Canards.

(A knock)

RUTA: Yes?

*(*CARDANO *enters.)*

*(*MORTMAIN *appears in another space, and tells the story.)*

MORTMAIN: Cardano had plastic surgery. His face is mine.

*(*CARDANO *uses* MORTMAIN's *voice.)*

CARDANO: (MORTMAIN's *voice*) More beautiful than ever.

RUTA: Darling...

(CARDANO *and* RUTA *embrace.*)

MORTMAIN: Ruta believes he is Mortmain, her husband.

CARDANO: (MORTMAIN's *voice*) Listen, Ruta. An agent came to see me at the interval.

RUTA: Yes...

CARDANO: (MORTMAIN's *voice*) We're going to America, Ruta. As far from the pigsty that is Lithuania as we can get. Mortmain's Realm of Shadows is going on tour: New York, Scranton, Toledo, Rapid City, Louisville. I've arranged to ship all the illusions. Our plane leaves tonight.

RUTA: But...

CARDANO: (MORTMAIN's *voice*) Get your coat.

RUTA: But we haven't packed. Our friends, at Les Trois Canards...

CARDANO: (MORTMAIN's *voice*) Fuck the three ducks.

(*They embrace again. She caresses his face. No reaction from her.*)

MORTMAIN: He copied my Realm of Shadows illusions, and fled to America. He took her with him.

CARDANO: (MORTMAIN's *voice*) I love you. I loved you ever since I first saw you.

RUTA: Mortmain...

(CARDANO *grabs her hand.*)

CARDANO: We're off! (*In his own Italian accent*) La vita nuova!

RUTA: What?

CARDANO: (MORTMAIN's *voice*) The new life.

(They're gone.)

MORTMAIN: Here in Louisville, I have caught up with him at last. Tonight, during his performance at the Majestic theater, I intend to murder him.

(An excited audience for the magic show appears,takes its places. In the audience, MORTMAIN.)

NARRATOR: *(In audience)* The Majestic Theater.

(CARDANO steps onstage.)

CARDANO: Cardano, as Mortmain, in tux and tails, is onstage. He beckons to the audience.

MORTMAIN: A volunteer comes up on stage—Mortmain, also in tux and tails.

(MORTMAIN joins CARDANO onstage.)

MORTMAIN & CARDANO: We are identical.

MORTMAIN: The true Mortmain goes behind the disappearance curtain. *(He holds a hand up in front of his eyes.)*

CARDANO: The false Mortmain raises his hand. *(He makes a magical gesture.)*

CARDANO: *Uno, due, tre!*

MORTMAIN: Mortmain reaches out, drags Cardano behind the curtain.

(CARDANO also holds a hand up in front of his eyes.)

CARDANO: Two pistol shots, then silence.

NARRATOR: *(In audience)* The curtain moves aside.

(MORTMAIN and CARDANO drop their hands slowly to their sides. Their heads hang lifelessly.)

NARRATOR: The two Mortmains lean against a wall,
stiff and dead, blood on their faces and clothes,
like a pair of dolls in tuxedos.

RUTA: Ruta stumbles onstage. She caresses the face of
one Mortmain, then the other. *(She does so.)* Mortmain
and Cardano. She no longer knows which is which.
Both men who loved her are dead. She's alone in a
strange country.

*(MORTMAIN and CARDANO are gone. An audience of
eastern European emigrés appears, fairly drunk.)*

NARRATOR: She gets a job singing in a cafe for eastern
European emigres.

*(RUTA sings her sad and passionate song. This time, there's a
driving music track behind it.)*

RUTA: *(Sings) Lume, lume, schwester welt
Ich werdas genug habenas welt...
Lume, lume...
Wenn ich kein brot pilius gatve
Und auch keinas kava balta
Welt, lume, lume.....*

*(An emigre, overcome with lust, grabs RUTA and pulls her
onto his lap. RUTA slaps him. Music ends.)*

NARRATOR: She's fired for fraternizing with the
customers. Now she works nights, cleaning a
downtown office building.

*(Emigre club patrons are all gone. RUTA kneels alone by a
bucket. Harsh fluorescent light.*

NARRATOR: Some nights she drinks a few glasses of
cheap Lithuanian wine, and falls asleep on the hallway
floor with her sponge for a pillow. Her dream is always
the same. She dreams she is back in the old country,
and her grandfather is holding her hand.

(RUTA's GRANDFATHER *enters. He walks over to where she sleeps, and as he does so, she rises up.*)

NARRATOR: They are in a field near Kaunas. A black stork flies low over the field, and in her dream, she can see it.

GRANDFATHER: This is where I go on Sunday, Ruta. When the others are in church. It's called the Ninth Fort. There once was a building here for soldiers. Its gone now. We are standing in a beautiful field full of wildflowers. I'll give you one.

(The GRANDFATHER *hands her a flower.)*

GRANDFATHER: The Nazis used this place as a killing ground in the war, long before you were born. They killed people, Jews and Lithuanians, and buried them. They're still here, deep under the earth. My wife—you never met her—was one of them. She had the same name as you. Ruta. She was twenty years old. That happened long ago, but I come here to remember... Lie down on the ground, Ruta, and you can hear the dead whispering to each other. Eternity is long, and they tell stories to pass the time.

*(*RUTA *listens. Her* GRANDFATHER *is gone.* DWAYNE *appears.)*

DWAYNE: Skambutis, baby. It's time.

RUTA: Who...who are you?

DWAYNE: Not your problem. Your problem is, you need a jump.

RUTA: Leave me alone... *(She is weeping.)*

DWAYNE: Cry your dead eyes out. I don't blame you. The planet's going downhill fast. We need to re-locate, big time. Take my hand.

(A Translation Machine. BIG BETTY *in shadow.* DWAYNE *puts* RUTA *behind the curtain of the machine. Strange sound*

*of the machine activating as lights flicker, then come up
again. DWAYNE and BIG BETTY are gone. Out from behind
the curtain steps VIVIAN, the next incarnation of Margo
Veil. A train, and a NARRATOR.)*

NARRATOR: Where are you now, Margo Veil? You're
on a train again, aren't you, Margo? Or is it Vivian?

(VIVIAN takes a seat on the train.)

NARRATOR: You're heading east, Vivian, once again
past Tuba City, past Bibo, past Albuquerque, under
a black sky. Don't you remember?

VIVIAN: Not really. All my memories feel like guests,
arriving by mistake at the wrong party. I need a drink.
They must have a club car on this train. Maybe a scotch
and soda...

BARMAN: Here's your drink, miss.

NARRATOR: Nobody in the club car but that priest,
staring out the window. Maybe he can offer some
consolation..

VIVIAN: Mind if I join you?

COMPANY: *(Sings softly, continuing under the dialogue
that follows)*
Jesus is on that mainline,
Tell him what you want,
Jesus is on that mainline,
Tell him what you want,
Jesus is on that mainline,
Tell him what you want,
You can call him up and tell him what you want
The line ain't never busy,
Tell him what you want...

REVEREND FORD: Look out there.

VIVIAN: It's night. I can't see anything.

REVEREND FORD: I can. Old lady under a bridge by the River Road. She lights a candle, mixes a pint of Jim Beam into a can of pineapple juice, peers out at the river through the reeds. She takes a sip, fog drifting in over the water... Neon through that fog, splotched and dim, like a watercolor rubbed with a damp rag. Shell. Gulf. Vacancy. Dunkin' Donuts, Tropical Fish and Aquarium Supplies, tank glows in the window, one huge angelfish gliding alone and slow in the green light. Turn and turn again under the cold stars.
I'm the Reverend Cletus Ford. Who are you?

VIVIAN: Vivian...Clay. I'm an acting teacher from Indianapolis, Indiana.

REVEREND FORD: Miss Clay, what are human beings made of? Salt water out of the sea, handful of...

VIVIAN: Skip that part. I've heard it somewhere before.

(The singing under stops.)

REVEREND FORD: When the great belt on the wheel of time slips loose, don't be afraid. The mountains tremble like beasts under the whip, and your chariot wheels spin hub deep in fire. Down, down, down...

CONDUCTOR: Indianapolis! Indianapolis, ten minutes.

VIVIAN: Gotta go.

(The REVEREND FORD *and his singers are gone. A line waiting to buy tickets for a movie. On line, Jimmy.)*

NARRATOR: You've got a life here, don't you Vivian? Vivian Clay. That's what it says on your office door in the theatre department at Indianapolis Community College. You even have a love life.

JIMMY: Yo!

NARRATOR: One of your students— Jimmy.

JIMMY: Hold my place, will ya?

(JIMMY *comes over to* VIVIAN.)

JIMMY: They're still not selling tickets. *(Looking at line)* Damn, this movie's popular.

VIVIAN: Hey, Jimmy?

JIMMY: Yeah? *(Seeing someone he knows)* Yo, Dwayne!

VIVIAN: Jimmy, I'm trying to talk to you. I been having funny dreams lately.

JIMMY: Funny?

VIVIAN: Not hah hah funny. Just funny. In each dream I'm in a different place, but there's always this guy. He looks familiar, but I can't remember how I know him—or even if I know him. Handsome guy, kind of hip looking.

JIMMY: What's he do?

VIVIAN: What do you mean what's he do?

JIMMY: In the dream.

VIVIAN: Nothing. He just kind of walks by.

JIMMY: You're losing it, Viv.

VIVIAN: Asshole.

JIMMY: Why you even telling me this? It's nothing.

VIVIAN: It's not nothing.

JIMMY: You're stressed. You need to smoke more dope.

VIVIAN: Jesus.... Jimmy?

JIMMY: Yeah?

VIVIAN: Am I gonna like this movie? What's it about?

JIMMY: Stuff blowing up, including helicopters and creatures dripping slime.

VIVIAN: I hate that shit. I am not a twelve year old boy.

JIMMY: Kidding. We went to see *X-Men 4*, this is my payback. Its an art film. However, it does have Edgar LeStrange in it, that guy who did *Feast of Blood*.

VIVIAN: Who else?

JIMMY: Margo Veil. She is so hot its criminal. She's a criminal offense. Pepsi saw it.

VIVIAN: Pepsi saw this picture? Its gotta be..

JIMMY: Pepsi is not dumb. He said it had sex, and a cool dream sequence. Made him cry.

VIVIAN: Pepsi is a...

MOVIE USHER: Immediate seating for *A Distant Candelabra*. *A Distant Candelabra* in theater three.

(A movie theater. A beam of white light. Cheesy orchestral underscoring. Over it, and in the beam of light, HEPSTEIN, *the second rate theatrical agent, and the original* MARGO VEIL, *"on film.")*

HEPSTEIN: Parents? I thought girls like you, they grew them in a vat in Minnesota.

MARGO: They said go to New York, Margo, give it a try, get it out of your system. Well, I tried.

HEPSTEIN: I guess you have. You know, I went to see *A Distant Candelabra*. It stunk. You stunk in it. Who wrote that thing?

MARGO: Arthur Vine's his name.

HEPSTEIN: Handsome?

MARGO: Some of the girls thought so...

HEPSTEIN: Artistic? Deep?

MARGO: Some of the girls...

(VIVIAN's attention is caught by a man passing in front of the screen, through the beam of white light. It's VINE.)

VIVIAN: Jimmy! That's him. Him— the guy who's been in my dreams.

JIMMY: You kidding me?

VIVIAN: He's leaving the theater! Gotta go!

(VIVIAN bolts from her seat. She's gone.)

JIMMY: Yo! Viv! I'll save your seat!

(The movie theater and JIMMY are gone. An office building lobby.)

VIVIAN: Nobody around. I'm sure he went into this office building.

NARRATOR: Isn't it curious, Vivian Clay? One moment you're with your boyfriend seeing *A Distant Candelabra*. Now, you're in the lobby of an anonymous office building, looking for a man who's been haunting your dreams. And you're all alone— except for the elevator operator.

(An elevator slides open. PROFESSOR HELEN AHRIMAN is at the controls.

AHRIMAN: Going up?

VIVIAN: I'm...I don't know. I'm looking for a man who just...

AHRIMAN: Mister Vine. Arthur Vine?

VIVIAN: I know that name. Somehow. Who's...

AHRIMAN: Step in. He got off on the top floor.

(VIVIAN does. The elevator starts to rise.)

AHRIMAN: I'm Professor Helen Ahriman.

VIVIAN: Excuse me. You're an elevator operator.

AHRIMAN: Just nights. Till I get back on my feet. I wouldn't send my parrot to that university. The entire archaeology department—pedantic puritanical

pederasts. They took away my library card. Fired me,
Sherry. Fired...

VIVIAN: My name's not Sherry. I'm Vivian. Vivian Clay.

AHRIMAN: Sherry, let me show you something...
Lithuanian. A marble carving of the spirit of change.

(AHRIMAN *takes out the statue of the owl-like demon.
The elevator hisses to a stop.*)

AHRIMAN: Touch its nose, and make a wish!

VIVIAN: I'll pass.

(*The elevator opens, and* VIVIAN *steps out.*)

AHRIMAN: Top floor. Last door on the right. Little bitch.

(AHRIMAN *and her elevator are gone.* VIVIAN *moves down
the hall, reading the names on the doors.*)

VIVIAN: Hyman Hepstein, theatrical agent; Lithuanian
Travel Services; Morlock Enterprises—

NARRATOR: What did that professor say, Vivian? Last
one on the right...

VIVIAN: Tanning Salon and Styling Academy.

NARRATOR: Go on, Vivian. Ring the bell.

(VIVIAN *does. DING*)

(*A Translation Parlor.* BIG BETTY *and* DWAYNE *as before.
She sits in a huge chair, with a pint of Night Train. She sings*
Let it Shine on Me *to herself.* DWAYNE *wears a Hawaiian
shirt, open to the navel. A Translation Machine, with
curtain. DING!*)

DWAYNE: Some living creature's out there. Do I...

BIG BETTY: It's late, Dwayne. And I have a feeling. I
feel....empty. Pointless. What does it matter, Dwayne?
One shell or another? We're repeating ourselves, here
in the Milky Way. I'm fading, Dwayne, translucent...

(DING!)

DWAYNE: Stop your metaphysical whining. Let's get this thing done.

(DWAYNE lets VIVIAN in.)

VIVIAN: 'Scuse me. I'm looking for...

BIG BETTY: I know you, Margo Veil.

VIVIAN: Margo Veil?

BIG BETTY: The soul...the soul is...I can smell it. Margo Veil. Still there. You've had so many jumps, you've forgotten. So many dreams. That itch brings you back to me, doesn't it?

VIVIAN: Actually, I'm looking for...

DWAYNE: She's hot. Tssss!

BIG BETTY: Excuse Dwayne. He's not himself this evening.

VIVIAN: The man I'm looking...

BIG BETTY: The itch. Your body doesn't seem to fit anymore. Dwayne, see if that potential client is still in back.

(DWAYNE peeks through a curtain.)

DWAYNE: She's sleeping. Like a baby.

BIG BETTY: You're in luck, Miss Veil. We have your original body available. Only slightly the worse for wear. Follow Dwayne.

VIVIAN: You're nuts! I'm out of here..

(VIVIAN tries to run, but DWAYNE grabs her.)

BIG BETTY: And Miss Veil, don't worry about our fee. Arthur Vine has paid for you already.

VIVIAN: *(Struggling in* DWAYNE'S *grip)* Arthur Vine.
Who's Arthur Vine? Who are you? *(To* DWAYNE*)*
And who the hell are you?

BIG BETTY: Dwayne, help her strip.

*(*DWAYNE *drags* VIVIAN, *kicking and screaming, behind the
curtain of the Translation Machine. They're gone.* BIG BETTY
*sips her Night Train. Strange sound of the Translation
Machine. The lights flicker, then brighten.)*

*(*MARGO VEIL *herself, in her original body, emerges from
behind the curtain.)*

BIG BETTY: How does it feel, Miss Veil? Body and soul
back together.

MARGO: O K, I guess. Where is he?

BIG BETTY: Arthur? He's on the terrace, waiting for you.
(She's gone.)

(The terrace. It's empty. MARGO *is alone. Lights of a great
city below.)*

MARGO: Arthur? Arthur? Arthur?

(A NARRATOR *appears.)*

NARRATOR: No one's here, Margo. Just you. Far below,
the lights of the city.

*(*MARGO *goes to the lip of the terrace, looks out.)*

MARGO: The lights! They're unbelievably beautiful.

NARRATOR: And then the terrace under you dissolves,
like smoke...

(Darkness, with MARGO *in a pulsing shaft of light.)*

MARGO: I'm falling...

NARRATOR: Down, down, down. Will the fall never
end? An owl-like creature flies by and disappears into

the darkness. Look, Margo. The lights of the city are closer now. Or are they?

(The shaft of light around MARGO *pulses more slowly, and then holds steady and bright.)*

NARRATOR & MARGO: And it seems to Margo Veil that she's falling slowly. Ever so slowly. She has time to notice the yellow moon, and the cold stars.
All the time in the world.

(The shaft of light fades on MARGO, *as the surrounding darkness brightens. The entire company appears around* MARGO.*)*

NARRATOR & MARGO: *(Sing)*
Let it shine on me
Let it shine on me
Let your light from the lighthouse shine on me
Let is shine on
Let it shine on
Let your light from the lighthouse shine on me

FULL COMPANY: I saw the beacon and I heard the bell
Let your light from the lighthouse shine on me
I got the message that no tongue can tell
Let your light from the lighthouse shine on me
Let it shine on me
Let it shine on me
Let your light from the lighthouse shine on me
Let it shine on
Let is shine on
Let your light from the lighthouse shine on me

(Someone flips off the reel-to-reel tape deck. The performers exit, one by one or in small groups. MARGO *remains alone onstage. The lights dim, then flicker. In the distance, the sound of an explosion, and another. A siren wails, far off. The lights go out.)*

END OF PLAY